Contents

Giant Animals Ahead 1
Blue Whale 6
Asian Elephant 10
Gaur 14
Himalayan Brown Bear 18
Indian Rhinoceros........................ 22
Reticulated Python 26
Sambar 30
Sarus Crane 34
Asian Water Monitor 38
Little Giants 42
Spot Them Here! 46
Fact Finder and Credits 47

Giant Animals Ahead

Some animals are small enough to hold in your hand, while others are so tall, you'd need a ladder just to pat their head! The animal kingdom is full of giant animals, living in thick forests, tall grasslands and deep oceans – some tall, some heavy, and all of them truly amazing. Some of them are gentle grazers, while others are hunters who need to chase their food – usually smaller animals.

The Thing About Being Large

Many large herbivores (plant-eating animals) such as elephants, rhinos and gaur spend most of their day eating grass, fruits and leaves to fuel their big bodies. Others, like the Himalayan brown bear are carnivores (meat-eating animals) and will eat just about anything – from wild berries to fish – depending on the season. Their large size can help them stay safe, find food or travel long distances.

Male sambar deer use their antlers to spar during mating season

How Do They Grow So Big?

Growing big takes time, space and a lot of food! Some animals are born large, while others grow slowly over time. Plant-eating animals often eat for hours each day to keep up their strength. On the other hand, meat-eating animals usually don't eat as often — but when they do, they need a big meal to keep them full! Being large in size also helps animals reach food others cannot, like leaves of tall trees or river plants.

A herd of elephants in Munnar, Kerala

Is It Better to Be to Big in the Wild?

Being huge can come with lots of advantages. Big animals often have strong muscles and special abilities to help them survive in the wild. Larger animals can scare off enemies and protect their young ones. It also makes solo survival easier for animals like rhinos and bears. But some large animals, such as gaur and elephants, like to stay in groups to find food and stay safe.

What Role Do They Play in Nature?

Their size isn't just for show – it is part of how they survive. Every big animal has a specific role to play in nature. These giants create paths through forests for smaller creatures or dig up the ground as they move. Whether it's clearing space for new plants or a big meat-eater keeping the animal numbers in check, their size is part of what makes them so important.

The sarus crane, found in Rajasthan

Blue Whale

Find Me Here!

In the Arabian Sea and the Bay of Bengal as well as off the Lakshadweep Islands, but you have to be very patient.

CRITTER STATS

Scientific name: *Balaenoptera musculus*
Size: 20–24 m – as long as two school buses!
Weight: 90,000 kg
Lifespan: 80–90 years
Habitat: off the Indian coast
Conservation status: endangered

Meet the blue whale, the largest animal on the planet! One special kind of blue whale lives in the Indian Ocean, which is slightly smaller than the one that lives in Antarctica. But despite their size, they are peaceful creatures, gliding quietly through the sea.

When blue whales swim near the surface and sunlight hits their skin, they shimmer with a blue glow – that's how they get their name!

Even though it's so big, the blue whale eats some of the smallest creatures in the sea, such as the tiny shrimp-like animal called krill.

The way a blue whale catches its food is also unique. It slurps in a mouthful of seawater and then pushes it out, trapping krill in brush-like plates in its mouth, called "baleen".

Blue whales are also extremely loud! They make deep, rumbling sounds. These sounds help them talk to other whales far away.

DID YOU KNOW?

Blue whale babies are called calves and they are born big! A newborn calf can be 7 to 8 m long – that is as long as your school van!

Milk guzzlers: blue whale babies drink up to 200 litres of milk every day. That's more than a whole bathtub full of milk!

Hold your breath! Blue whales can hold their breath for up to 30 minutes underwater before they come up to breathe.

Asian Elephant

Find Me Here!
National parks such as Kaziranga and Manas in Assam and Mudumalai in Tamil Nadu are great places to spot them.

CRITTER STATS
Scientific name: *Elephas maximus*
Size: 6–11.5 feet – as tall as a house!
Weight: 3,000–5,000 kg
Lifespan: 45–48 years in captivity
Habitat: forests and grassland
Conservation status: endangered

The Asian elephant is the largest land animal and one of the most beloved animals in the country. This giant is found across India's forests, grasslands and even near tea plantations. A full-grown male can be taller than a basketball hoop and weigh more than a truck!

An elephant's trunk – a long nose and an upper lip rolled into one – is a super tool! With it, they can grab and lift objects, spray water and smell faraway scents.

Elephants live in herds led by the oldest female, called a matriarch. She remembers everything – where to find food, water and safe paths.

Baby elephants weigh about 100 kg at birth – that's heavier than a big fridge! They stay close to their moms and aunts, who help take care of them.

Elephants talk to each other using rumbles, trumpeting sounds and body movements.

They also use their feet to pick up vibrations in the ground, which helps them sense danger nearby and find their herd.

 DID YOU KNOW?

Elephants love to stay near water as they need to drink a lot of it. They enjoy taking mud baths to cool down and protect their skin from insects.

Elephants can sleep lying down or even standing up, and they usually nap for just 4 hours a day.

Great recall! Elephants have great memory. They can even recognise themselves in mirrors – just like humans and dolphins!

Gaur

Find Me Here!
In sanctuaries such as Kanha and Bandhavgarh in Madhya Pradesh and Nagarahole and Bandipur in Karnataka.

CRITTER STATS
Scientific name: *Bos gaurus*
Size: almost 7 feet – taller than most adults!
Weight: 650–1,500 kg
Lifespan: 30 years
Habitat: Western and Eastern Ghats
Conservation status: vulnerable

Also known as the Indian bison, the gaur is India's heaviest wild animal on land. With its strong body and enormous horns, they're the heavyweight champions of the forest! A fully grown male can weigh more than ten adult humans put together.

All gaurs have curved horns that rise up and then curl in.

The horns are black at the tips, and help in defending their herd and in fighting when two males compete.

They eat a lot of plants every day and love relaxing near salt licks – these are natural spots where the soil is rich in minerals.

Even though they're huge, gaurs are usually very shy. When they're feeling scared or threatened, they can attack their enemies with great strength and surprising speed!

Have you ever stamped your feet when angry? Well, gaurs do it too!

If they're angry or alert, they may stomp the ground or flick their tail. That's the sign for the humans around to quickly exit the scene!

DID YOU KNOW?

High jumps – gaur can jump up to 6 feet in the air, even with their heavy bodies!

Gaurs have a low-pitched "moo", very different from the sound a cow makes!

Powerful beasts: tigers are the only animals who can sometimes take down a healthy adult gaur, proving how strong these forest bulls are.

Himalayan Brown Bear

Find Me Here!

In Ladakh, Himachal Pradesh and Uttarakhand. Best seen at the Great Himalayan National Park.

CRITTER STATS

Scientific name: *Ursus arctos isabellinus*
Size: 7 feet tall when standing on two legs!
Weight: 250–350 kg
Lifespan: 20–30 years in the wild
Habitat: meadows, forests in the Himalayas
Conservation status: critically endangered

Say hello to the Himalayan brown bear, one of the largest land animals in the Himalayas. These powerful creatures live high up in the mountains, where it gets very cold and the land is often rocky and steep. But these animals are built for this landscape!

The Himalayan brown bear is easy to spot with its thick, shaggy coat that ranges from light brown to dark chocolate colour. Its fur helps keep it warm in chilly mountain air.

It has a big head, strong teeth and large paws with claws — perfect for digging through the snow or rocky ground.

Himalayan brown bears are omnivores, so they eat both plants and animals. They love to feed on roots, fruits and berries, insects, ants and rats, along with smaller animals like sheep.

When the winter cold sets in, this bear simply goes to sleep. This long winter sleep of 5 to 7 months is called hibernation.

 DID YOU KNOW?

Bear babies, called cubs, are born in the den during hibernation. At birth, they are the size of a squirrel!

Bears love to eat honey and will tear apart trees or rocks to find beehives, all in the search of a sweet fix!

Even though they look slow and sleepy, Himalayan brown bears can run fast, swim well and climb rocks.

Indian Rhinoceros

Find Me Here!

National parks and wildlife sanctuaries such as Manas in Assam. Best place to see – Kaziranga!

CRITTER STATS

Scientific name: *Rhinoceros unicornis*
Size: almost 6 feet – as tall as a refrigerator!
Weight: 1,800–2,500 kg
Lifespan: 35–40 years
Habitat: tall, wet grasslands
Conservation status: vulnerable

The Indian rhinoceros, or greater one-horned rhinoceros, is the second largest mammal in India. It's horn might look like a hard bone, but it's made of keratin – the same stuff that makes up your nails and hair. It may look fearsome, but rhinos use their horn only in defence, not attack.

The rhino's skin is so thick that it forms large folds. These folds help protect the rhino from bites, scratches and heat!

It may look like it's got armour on, but the rhino's skin is very sensitive. Rhinos love rolling around in mud puddles to keep cool in the summer months and prevent bug bites.

Indian rhinos are mostly calm and shy and prefer to live alone. They also leave behind marks using poop and urine to tell other rhinos, "This is my space!"

This is a creature of habit. Rhinos walk the same paths regularly and also poop at a common spot – much like our public toilets!

DID YOU KNOW?

Swimming giants: rhinos are also great swimmers and can even walk underwater through rivers and swamps!

Blurry-eyed – rhinos can't see very well but they have a great sense of smell and hearing.

At birth, baby rhinos weigh about 60 to 70 kg – almost as much as a grown man!

Reticulated Python

Find Me Here!
They are only found in the wild in the Nicobar Islands.

CRITTER STATS
Family: *Malayopython reticulatus*
Size: 20 feet – as long as a bus!
Weight: 100–270 kg
Lifespan: 20–25 years in the wild
Habitat: humid forests
Conservation status: least concern

The reticulated python is the longest and third-heaviest snake in the world! This impressive snake slithers through rainforests, grasslands and even in rivers. With its shiny skin and massive body, it's one of the most eye-catching and powerful snakes in the wild.

Its body is covered in scales, with diamond shapes in gold, black and white, helping it blend into the forest.

This giant snake is a carnivore, which means it eats only meat. Small pythons snack on birds, rats and lizards. But big ones can eat animals like pigs and monkeys!

Even though it doesn't have venom, this snake is a master of strength. It uses its powerful body to wrap around its prey and squeeze tightly until the animal can't breathe.

Reticulated pythons live alone and come out mostly at night. They love to hide in caves, under logs, or near water. They're also excellent swimmers.

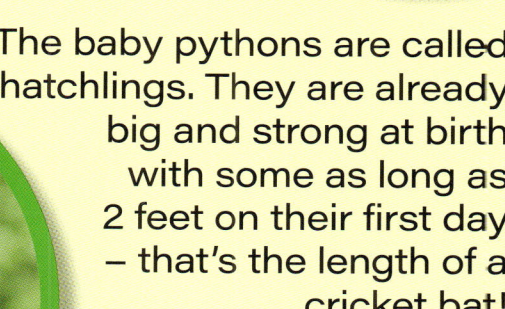

The baby pythons are called hatchlings. They are already big and strong at birth with some as long as 2 feet on their first day – that's the length of a cricket bat!

DID YOU KNOW?

Natural glow – their skin looks like a rainbow in sunlight.

Tummy's full – after a huge meal, a reticulated python might not eat again for weeks!

Pythons never chew their food – they swallow everything whole, bones and all!

Sambar

Find Me Here!

In most national parks. Periyar National Park in Kerala and Pench National Park in Madhya Pradesh are hotspots.

CRITTER STATS

Family: *Rusa unicolor*
Size: 5–6 feet – as high as a big door!
Weight: 130–270 kg
Lifespan: 20–26 years
Habitat: forests and bush land
Conservation status: vulnerable

India's largest deer is a shy giant with big ears, strong legs and shaggy brown coats. You are most likely to spot one quietly standing still among the trees – despite their size, sambar are experts at hiding in plain sight!

They have thick, rough fur that protects them from the rain, cold and scratches from bushes. It is dark brown and the neck has a little mane!

Male deer have large antlers with three sharp points, which they use to show off their strength, especially when they're looking for a partner.

Sambar deer are plant-eaters (herbivores) and they aren't picky! They munch on leaves, grass, fruit, twigs and tree bark.

They're also really good swimmers! If there's a river or lake nearby, they don't mind jumping in to cool off or swim to safety. They also jump into water when chased by predators such as dholes.

DID YOU KNOW?

Heat-busters – they love taking mud baths to cool off and get rid of itchy bugs.

When sambar sense danger, they give a loud call – almost like a honking trumpet – to warn others nearby.

They have a special way of chewing, called chewing the cud, where they bring back swallowed food from their stomach and chew it again to digest it.

Sarus Crane

Find Me Here!

In the northern plains of India, especially near wetlands in states like Uttar Pradesh and Rajasthan.

CRITTER STATS

Family: *Grus antigone*
Length: almost 6 feet – taller than most grown-ups!
Weight: 5–10 kg
Lifespan: 40 years in captivity
Habitat: wetlands, marshes and fields
Conservation status: least concern

Meet the sarus crane, the tallest flying bird on Earth! These birds love being near water and are often spotted in rice fields, where they help farmers by eating insects and snails.

Their long legs help them walk on wetlands and their long, pointed beaks help them poke around in the muddy water to find tasty snacks.

Sarus cranes are expert dancers and this talent is on display when they pair up to make babies! When they dance, they jump, flap their wings, bow, spin and trumpet away.

These birds are famous for being loving and loyal and they usually stay with one partner for life.

Sarus crane chicks are cute balls of yellowish-brown fluff – but they can walk just a few hours after they're born!

They have light grey feathers and their bright red heads make them stand out.

 DID YOU KNOW?

A lucky charm – it is believed that if you spot them, they'll bring you good luck and happiness.

When fully open, the sarus crane's wings, stretch 8 feet – that's the length of a surfboard!

Their loud calls can be heard from far away – it's how they keep in touch with their partner or family when they're apart.

Asian Water Monitor

Find Me Here!
In Assam, West Bengal and Kerala near rivers, swamps and wetlands. You might even spot one around cities, near canals!

CRITTER STATS

Family: *Varanus salvator*
Length: 4–6 feet long – as long as a bed!
Weight: 15–40 kg
Lifespan: 25 years in captivity
Habitat: near rivers, swamps and wetlands
Conservation Status: least concern

Have you ever seen a lizard so big it looks like a mini dinosaur? Meet the Asian water monitor, one of the largest lizards in the world! They have dark, scaly skin with yellow or white spots, helping them blend into their natural surroundings. These spots fade as they grow older.

Water monitors can live on land and in water. On land, their claws and legs help them run really fast. They're great swimmers too!

Their long tails work like paddles, helping them slice through water. They can hold their breath for up to 30 minutes!

They love to eat fish, frogs, birds, rodents and crabs, but also like to snack on dead animals. They can even eat young crocs and their eggs!

Monitors have a forked tongue, just like snakes. They flick it out to smell the air and find out what's around them.

DID YOU KNOW?

Dig deep – they often dig burrows near water to rest and hide, just like rabbits!

Expert climbers: with their sharp claws, Asian water monitors are great at climbing trees and rocks, in search of food or just to sit in the sun.

These lizards are shy and stay away from people. They may hiss or whip their tails, but they'd rather run away than fight!

Little Giants

Himalayan Golden Birdwing
CRITTER STATS
Family: *Troides aeacus*
Wingspan: up to 19.4 cm – as wide as your lunchbox!
Weight: only 5–10 g
Found in: Uttarakhand, Sikkim, Arunachal Pradesh
Conservation status: least concern

Black Giant Squirrel
CRITTER STATS
Family: *Ratufa bicolor*
Size: just short of a metre
Weight: 1–1.5 kg
Found in: north-east India
Conservation status: near threatened

Indian Crested Porcupine
CRITTER STATS
Family: *Hystrix indica*
Size: 3 feet – as long as an umbrella!
Weight: 11–18 kg
Found in: across India except the northeast
Conservation status: least concern

Not all giants are big and neither do all stomp and roar loudly. Some live in the forest in more surprising ways. These are the little giants of the animal world. Get ready to meet these smaller animals, which are record holders in their own right!

Himalayan Golden Birdwing

The golden birdwing is the largest butterfly in India! Its wings are a mix of black and bright yellow spots. When it flaps its wings, it looks like a floating flower!

This butterfly is a big fan of sweet treats! It loves drinking nectar (a juice that flowers make) from bright flowers like hibiscus and lantana. It also helps with pollination, which means spreading flower seeds (called pollen) from one place to another. This makes new plants grow!

Black Giant Squirrel

This is one of the biggest squirrels in the world! It is known for its super-strong legs and amazing jumping skills.

Unlike other squirrels, these don't like to come down to the ground very often. They're super shy and love their leafy homes high above.

Indian Crested Porcupine

Meet the largest rodent in India! The porcupine's body is covered in quills, which are actually special hairs made of keratin – just like your nails! Some of these quills are soft and short, but others are long, sharp and hollow, especially the ones on its back. They rattle their quills and tail as their warning or run backwards to poke you!

DID YOU KNOW?

This butterfly is called "birdwing" because of its size and how it flies – almost like a bird!

They can leap more than 30 feet in one jump – that's like jumping across a whole classroom!

Unlike other kinds of porcupines, Indian crested porcupines can't shoot their quills arrow-style, but they sure can use them for protection.

Spot Them Here!

Follow the pug marks to find some of the best places to spot India's amazing wildlife! Animals such as the Indian crested porcupine and sambar live across many regions of India.

Fact Finder

"Blue Whale." *Whale Watching Handbook*, https://wwhandbook.iwc.int/en/species/blue-whale.

"Asian Elephant." *WWF*, https://www.worldwildlife.org/species/asian-elephant.

"*Elephas maximus*." *Animal Diversity Web*, https://animaldiversity.org/accounts/Elephas_maximus/.

"*Bos gaurus* (Gaur)." *India Biodiversity Portal*, https://indiabiodiversity.org/species/show/226713.

"Himalayan Brown Bear." *Bear Conservation*, http://www.bearconservation.org.uk/himalayan-brown-bear/.

"Why Do Rhinos Have Horns?" *Discover Wildlife*, https://www.discoverwildlife.com/animal-facts/why-do-rhinos-have-horns.

"Reticulated Python." *Encyclopaedia Britannica*, https://www.britannica.com/animal/reticulated-python.

"*Rusa unicolor* (Sambar)." *India Biodiversity Portal*, https://indiabiodiversity.org/species/show/253962.

"Sarus Crane." *Wildlife Institute of India*, https://wii.gov.in/nmcg/priority-species/birds/sarus-crane.

"*Grus antigone*." *Animal Diversity Web*, https://animaldiversity.org/accounts/Grus_antigone/.

"Elvis, Asian Water Monitor." *Legasea Aquarium*, https://legaseaaquarium.com/pages/elvis-asian-water-monitor.

"*Ratufa bicolor*." *Animal Diversity Web*, https://animaldiversity.org/accounts/Ratufa_bicolor/.

Credits

Writer: Abhidha

Designer: Abhishikta Dutt

Picture Credits

iStockphoto: Deer stock photo by Robbie Ross, #904053098; Munnar landscapes and elephants stock photo by Aravindh Rengaraj, #1139491207; Sarus crane or Grus antigone bird portrait or closeup with full wingspan or flapping behavior in winter morning at keoladeo national park bharatpur rajasthan india asia stock photo by Sourabh Bharti, #1443245623; Blue Whales - Sri Lanka April 2012 stock photo by eco2drew, #637250780; Blue Whale, Sri Lanka, Indian Ocean stock photo by eco2drew, #638034848; The blue whale (Balaenoptera musculus) is a marine mammal belonging to the baleen whales (Mysticeti) and sometimes found in the Monterey Bay, California. stock photo by Gerald Corsi, #1370988710; Blue whale diving deep underwater stock photo by pryzmat, #2170573114; Elephant in India stock photo by sabirmallick, #487153031; Young elephant eating banana in nature stock photo by psisa, #628138002; THAILAND SURIN ELEPHANT ROUND UP FESTIVAL stock photo by urf, #641488484; Full body face of asian elephant isolated white background stock photo by suriya silsaksom, #853731156; Minneriya Elephant Gathering stock photo by Gayan Pushpakumara, #1922703858; Gaur stock photo by Kantapatp, #164660454; Wild Indian Gaur in Kanha National Park stock photo by milehightraveler, #180706609; Gaur in the dark and white background stock photo by anankkml, #586183786; Wild male Gaur or Indian Bison or bos gaurus a danger animal or beast with blurred spotted deer or chital axis deer in foreground at landscape of bandhavgarh national park forest madhya pradesh india stock photo by Sourabh Bharti, #2153224736; The gaur (Bos gaurus) is a bovine native to South Asia and Southeast Asia. stock photo by Banu R, #2161025215; The gaur (Bos gaurus) is a bovine native to South Asiaand Southeast Asia. stock photo by Banu R, #2161025225; A wild herd of Indian gaur grazing next to a forest at Manas National Park, Assam, India stock photo by Soumabrata Moulick, #2169494012; Portrait of a gaur well isolated from the background at Manas National Park, Assam, India stock photo by Soumabrata Moulick, #2169494013; Himalayan Brown Bear Duo stock photo by Jay Dee, #1341513956; Himalayan brown bear (Ursus arctos isabellinus) stock photo by Artush, #842823196; Sleepy Hollow stock photo by tepic, #94071411; Himalayan brown bear (Ursus arctos isabellinus) stock photo by Artush, #842823160; Himalayan brown bear by Artush, #842823196; Sleeping Himalayan brown bear on rocks by dmf87, #1386059336; Greater One-horned Rhinoceros by Utopia_88, #612640066; "nGreater One-horned Rhinoceros, Royal Bardia National Park, Nepal stock photo by Al Carrera, #1343168689; Mother + calf Indian Rhino, Rhinoceros unicornis, Kaziranga Rhino, Rhinoceros unicornis, Kaziranga by Liz Leyden, #1485549546; One Horned Rhino by Ranzi Photography, #1618540293; An adult rhino by Soumabrata Moulick, #2168097967; Vertical close-up portrait of a greater one-horned rhinoceros bySoumabrata Moulick, #2172470594; Reticulated python head, front view stock photo by RibeirodosSantos, #476833864; Reticulated Python by Mark Kostich, #486925950; Reticulated Python stock photo by Mark Kostich, #487506120; Python snake stock photo by BenGrasser, #503860474; Reticulated Python snake isolated on black background. stock photo by dwi septiyana, #1373090847; Reticulated by fototrips, #1994097967; Juvenile Sambar Deer. stock photo by manx_in_the_world, #172431957; Wild male Sambar deer by Sourabh Bharti, #2208472737; Sambar deer with grass on antlers stock photo by anankkml, #2205083185; Sarus Crane (Grus Antigone) stock photo by ScratchArt, #179136861; Sarus crane by Sourabh Bharti, #1929577909; Sarus Crane at its Nest. stock photo by eROMAZe, #2200524967; The water monitor. stock photo by TTshutter, #181180994; The water monitor by chutarat sae-khow, #1083245542; Asian water monitor lizard in lake; looking at camera, tongue extended. stock photo by DGHayes, #2211554617; Asian water monitor lizard DGHayes, #2211554622; Golden Birdwing butterfly reproduction stock photo by svehlik, #538452667; A golden birdwing butterfly by Satakorn, #2208303773; Black giant squirrel stock photo by thawats, #474003346; Black Giant Squirrel stock photo by AmitRane1975, #693272290; Black Giant Squirrel Pair by AmitRane1975, #693272298; black giant squirrel by Soumabrata Moulick, #2200120711; Porcupine stock photo by Kyslynskyy, #481987080; Spiky Indian Crested Porcupine by Kamadie, #1304184115; A Porcupine by heckepics, #2199036954.

Pexels: Wild Elephants Enjoying Water in Sri Lanka Wilderness by Sergey Polyakov; Photo Of Elephants On Grass by Katie Hollamby; Close-up of a Python by Jeffry S.S.; Deer on Green Grass Field by Elina Sazonova; Sarus Crane Bird in Close-Up Photography by Rutpratheep Nilpechr; Lizard in Close Up Photography by NSU MON; Close-up of a Golden Birdwing Butterfly on Flowers by Pon Thhao.

Unsplash: big fish during daytime by Venti Views; a couple of elephants are standing in the water by Getty Images; a rhinoceros standing in a field with trees in the background by Getty Images; a close up of a snake on a bed by David Clode; a couple of animals that are standing in the grass Sambar Deer (Vulnerable species) by Hongbin; a deer by Rijul Chaturvedi; a couple of deer standing next to each other Sambar deer by Tim Promwanna; A lizard that is standing on a log by Peter Brooker.

Wikimedia Commons: Balaenoptera musculus by anim1754 NOAA Photo Library; Male camp elephant (Elephas maximus indicus, captive) bathes self in Moyar River, Mudumalai National Park, Tamilnadu, India by Timothy A. Gonsalves; The Brown Bear family; grazing in the fields and mostly dependent on grasses in Northern Pakistan by Uzair Ahmad; Himalayan brown bear - Kugti Wildlife Sanctuary by Niazulkhan; Čeština: medvěd plavý v Zoo Hluboká / English: Himalayan brown bear in Zoo Hluboka by Zoo Hluboka; Sambar Deer @ Tadoba Lake by Karunakanth; Sambar (Rusa unicolor) female, Bardiya National Park, Nepal by Charles J. Sharp; Indian Sarus Crane (Grus antigone) performing its courtship ritual by Ad031259; Sarus Crane (Grus antigone) by Rupal Vaidya; Migration season at Keoladeo National Park, Bharatpur, Rajasthan. Feb 2020 by Nagarjun; Sarus crane (Grus antigone), Salai, UP, India by Charles J. Sharp; Head of varanus salvator close up by Μαυλάνα; Asian water monitor by Tisha Mukherjee; Troides aeacus aeacus Golden Birdwing pupa Chaiyaphum by Len Worthington; Troides aeacus aeacus by Len Worthington; Golden Birdwing, female, upperwing by Adalbert Seitz (ed.); Golden Birdwing Larvae by Len Worthington; Troides aeacus formosanus female by Peellden; The black giant squirrel or Malayan giant squirrel by Chintamanivk; Taken at Rema-Kalenga Wildlife Sanctuary by Sarikasiraj; Hystrix indica by Johannes Maximilian.

iNaturalist: Indian Rhinoceros (Rhinoceros unicornis) by n_armstrong; Indian Rhinoceros (Rhinoceros unicornis) by Tristan Jobin; Reticulated Python (Malayopython reticulatus) by Samuel GUIRAUDOU.

Map: Syailendra Gupta Muliawan, India Vectors by Vecteezy.

First published by Juggernaut Books 2025

Text copyright © Juggernaut Books 2025

10 9 8 7 6 5 4 3 2 1

P-ISBN: 9789353459055

E-ISBN: 9789353458072

All rights reserved. No part of this publication may be reproduced, transmitted, or stored in a retrieval system in any form or by any means without the written permission of the publisher.

Printed at Nutech Print Services - India